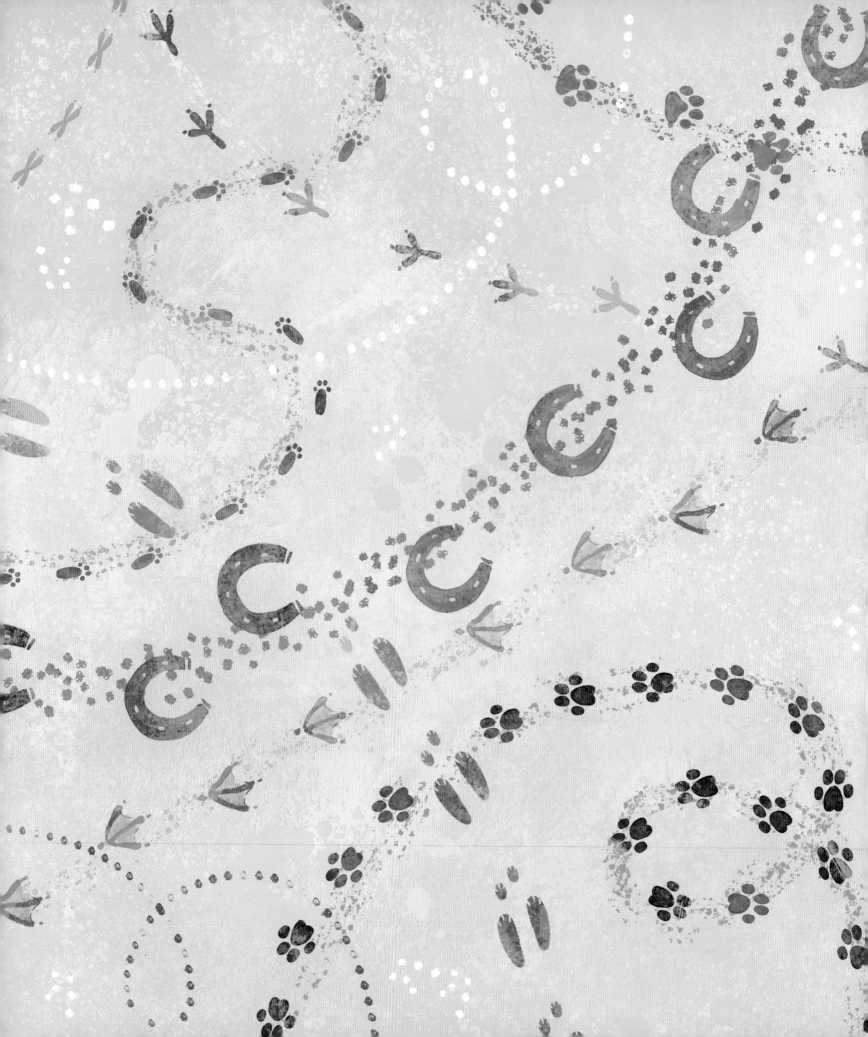

To my dog, Cherry, for her companionship and to all pets around the world. **A.C.**

First published in Great Britain 2023 by Red Shed, part of Farshore
An imprint of HarperCollins*Publishers*
1 London Bridge Street, London SE1 9GF
www.farshore.co.uk

HarperCollins*Publishers*
Macken House,
39/40 Mayor Street Upper,
Dublin 1, D01 C9W8 Ireland

Text copyright © HarperCollins*Publishers* 2023
Illustrations copyright © Anna Chernyshova 2023
The illustrator has asserted her moral rights.

ISBN 978 1 4052 9973 2
Printed in the UK by Bell and Bain Ltd, Glasgow.
001

Consultancy by Penny Graham BVMS MRCVS.

A CIP catalogue record for this title is available from the British Library.

Stay safe online. Any website addresses listed in this book are correct at the time of going to print. However, Farshore is not responsible for content hosted by third parties. Please be aware that online content can be subject to change and websites can contain content that is unsuitable for children. We advise that all children are supervised when using the internet.

FSC
www.fsc.org

MIX
Paper | Supporting responsible forestry
FSC™ C007454

Lucy Beech

Anna Chernyshova

Pick a Pet

RED SHED

Pets are all so **different!**

Some are big,

some are small.

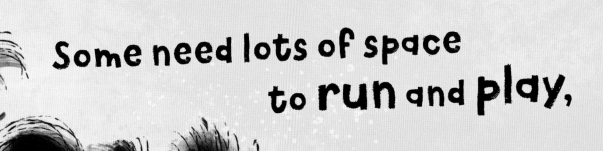

Some need lots of space to **run** and **play**,

and others are **super snuggly.**

What do they all have in common?
They **ALL** need someone to love them
and look after them properly!

Imagine if you could pick a pet.
Which one could be right for you?

Do you have space for a great BIG pet?

A **Saint Bernard dog** is a gentle giant who will love to be part of your family. That's if your home is big enough . . . and you don't mind a slobbery kiss!

Meet the **Maine Coon**, a massive cat with a huge personality to match. It's fluffy, cuddly and loves lots of room to clown around and play.

You can't keep a pony in your house! It needs a field and shelter. Ponies come in lots of sizes – **Shetlands** are one of the smallest (and even they can be just over one metre tall!).

Or perhaps a small pet would fit better?

You can keep **caterpillars** in a tank with plenty of leaves to eat, and wait for them to turn into . . . beautiful **butterflies**. Then you can set them free.

Mice like to be with their friends so they can play together.

How about a colony of **ants**? It's amazing to see how they live, work and play together, tunnelling into the sand.

Could you keep up with a **fast, lively** pet?

Zoom! **Greyhounds** are the fastest dogs around, though they also love a nap.

A bouncy, speedy **border collie** needs lots of long walks . . . or runs!

Choose a **tarantula** for something a bit different. It can whizz across walls and ceilings on its eight hairy legs – so keep it in a large tank with a lid.

Or would you pick a pet that's slooooow?

A **tortoise** plods around outdoors and needs a warm shelter too. You might see it climb rocks or burrow in soil . . . slowly.

Ducks and **ducklings** waddle and swim around a bit faster, but if you have a pond and don't mind the noise then they could suit you.

Don't expect speed from a **millipede**, even though it can have hundreds of legs.

Pick a **basset hound** for a dog that's very friendly and won't mind if you take your time on walks.

Snoozing is one of a **cat's** favourite habits, whether it's on a bed, on a windowsill or on your lap.

Do you dream of **winning** **competitions** with your pet?

Would your **cockapoo** win the dog with the waggiest tail award?

BEST IN SHOW

WAGGIEST TAIL

You and your **pony** could try different races.

SMARTEST

Brushing a **Siamese cat's** silky fur will help it shine at the cat show.

MOST ELEGANT

Maybe you'll be a winner at training your dog. **Irish setters** are intelligent so can be easy to train.

Or do you just want a **best friend** to play with?

Rats like to play with other rats but can learn to play with people too. Just remember to get to know them well first.

Guinea pigs love to play with you. They whistle when they're excited. Squeeee!

There are hundreds of types of **dogs** in the world and they're all special in their own way. Have you seen any dogs that might fit in with your family?

If your family are happy with a **noisy** pet, then choose one of these!

Squawk

Pick a **parrot** if you want a loud, chatty pet. They are clever and can copy people's words.

Crickets make a noise by rubbing their wings together. They chirp more when it's warm.

A **cockerel** will wake up the whole family with his rowdy morning call.

Woof!

Cock-a-doodle-doo!

Tiny **chihuahuas** can have a BIG bark, especially if they're anxious or lonely.

PSSST! By the way, how noisy are you? Loud or sudden sounds can upset pets, so be careful where you make a racket.

Shhhh! If a **quiet** pet sounds better, choose one of these . . .

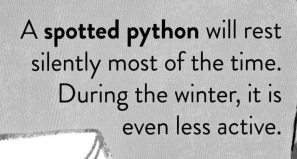

A **spotted python** will rest silently most of the time. During the winter, it is even less active.

Fish are about as quiet as a pet can be. It's relaxing to watch them swimming about. Don't forget to keep their tank clean.

Choose a **French bulldog** if you don't like lots of woofing – it's one of the quietest dogs.

Gentle **rabbits** make soft sounds, so you don't have to worry about them disturbing your neighbours!

How about a **furry** pet to groom and cuddle?

An **Old English sheepdog** has so much fur! Giving it a bath is fun, but hard work.

This silky **Persian cat** needs lots of brushing to keep its fur *purr*-fect.

Perhaps pick a herd of adorable **alpacas** . . . if you have a big field!

Be gentle if you want to stroke a super-soft **chinchilla**. These daytime sleepers run around at night.

Or would you choose a smooth, sleek pet?

Most rats have hairy coats to protect them, but a **Sphynx rat** is naked. Take care to keep yours warm.

Do you love cats but have allergies? You could pick a **Sphynx cat**. It has smooth skin with hardly any hair.

A **rainbow land crab's** shell is smooth, but watch out for its strong, sharp claws!

Snakes are slimy, right? Wrong! Their scaly skin is smooth and dry. Make sure you keep your **corn snake** warm and dry at the right temperature and humidity (moisture level).

Would your perfect pet stand out in a crowd?

Spot the **Dalmatian!** It's an eye-catching pet that needs loads of exercise every day.

A **rainbow lorikeet** lives up to its name – just look at those colourful feathers! This chatty bird will want to play and spend lots of time with you.

This busy **Bengal cat** has leopard-print fur. A cat cleans its fur with its tongue.

Male **betta fish** like to be the boss. They have bright, frilly fins and tails and have to be kept on their own in case they fight.

Or might you pick a pet that's great at hiding?

Where are you? **Leopard geckos** are brilliant at disguising themselves among stones!

A **chameleon** needs very special care. It can be shy and changes colour to hide when it gets stressed (which is a lot).

A **stick insect** hides among twigs and looks like . . . a stick!

And a **leaf insect** hides in the leaves and looks like . . . a green leaf!

Could you teach your pet special skills?

Sing or whistle to your chirpy pet **budgies** and they'll sing or whistle back.

How about teaching your friendly **golden retriever** to fetch balls . . .

. . . or shake hands?

A **ferret** is intelligent and will love playing and doing tricks. But watch out – it may bite.

Perhaps try teaching your bouncy **border terrier** to leap through hoops?

Most dogs love attention and are keen to learn, especially if you reward them with pats, praise and treats.

Do you have time to give a cheeky pet extra attention?

Cats love to scratch things to keep their claws healthy. A scratching post helps stop them damaging things.

Most **dogs** will gobble up your food if they get the chance, but take care as some human foods can make them ill.

Puppies can chew furniture, toys . . . almost anything. Give them chew toys and try not to leave them alone with things you care about.

A **hamster** is really good at escaping! Make sure its cage is safely closed.

Would you like to take photos of your pet? These ones have fabulous faces . . .

Watch your **hamster** pop food into its cheek pouches – keeping it safe to eat later!

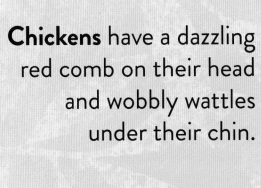

A **cory fish** looks like it has whiskers!

Chickens have a dazzling red comb on their head and wobbly wattles under their chin.

If your **dog** sticks its tongue out, the chances are it is hot – not being rude! Dogs pant to cool down.

A **bearded dragon** is a lizard with a 'beard' of spiky scales around its neck. Look at that big smile. It might even wave to you.

A **cockatiel** has a splendid head crest and will love you to stroke its rosy cheek.

...and these pets have tremendous tails!

Take care of your **crested gecko**. If it feels stressed or scared, its tail can drop off.

You can groom and plait a **horse's** thick tail, but always stand to the side in case it kicks.

A **rabbit's** tail is very soft, but a rabbit doesn't like its tail being touched.

This terrific tail is long and strong – it helps the **rat** to balance as it climbs.

Which end of a **worm** is its tail? Clue: it'll wriggle around your wormery head-first!

When the **red-lace guppy** swims, its tail flutters like a fantastic fan.

Come and play! A dog wags its tail to tell you it's excited, like this happy **cocker spaniel**.

A **peacock** is best left to expert pet keepers . . . but its tail feathers are spectacular.

Caring for your pet

If you are lucky enough to pick a pet in real life, don't forget that looking after your animal friend is a big responsibility. You need to provide it with a suitable home, the right food, and make sure it gets injections and health checks from a vet.

Each pet has its own unique needs: whether it is being kept alone or with a friend, needing long walks, or daily or weekly cleaning. It's important to know what your pet needs before you bring it home.

We love being with friends

Keep my tank clean

We need just the right temperature

There are also laws about what animals you can buy and keep as pets. The best thing to do is check with an expert before you choose one, and find out how to take care of it. You might be able to rehome an abandoned pet, so visit your local rescue centre to see if there's one that's right for you.

And don't worry if you can't have a pet. Perhaps you could ask to play with a friend's or neighbour's pet. Or how about you make your own special rock pet or cuddle a soft toy animal.

Find out more

Alpacas
Alpacas need lots of outside space and are happiest in groups – they can get lonely by themselves.

Birds
Birds need space to spread their wings and should generally get regular sunlight and fresh air.

Cats
Cats spend a lot of time sleeping – usually around 15 hours per day. Make sure they have a comfy bed!

Caterpillars
Caterpillars need to eat a lot to get ready to become butterflies!

Chickens
Chickens need a warm, dry place to roost (rest or sleep), and outdoor space that is fenced off to protect them from wild animals.

Chinchillas
Chinchillas' teeth are growing all the time – they need lots of things to chew on to make sure they don't get too long!

Crabs
Crabs need a home where they can choose between water and dry land – make sure they have plenty of fresh water and some sand.

Dogs
Dogs are generally playful and active. They enjoy the company of other dogs as well as forming strong social bonds with humans.

Ducks
Ducks need access to fresh, clean water at all times. Their feathers are completely waterproof – useful for diving to find food!

Ferrets
Ferrets are curious and so love exploring and chewing on objects. Keep them in a safe, secure environment.

Fish

The bigger the tank you can find the better! Make sure your fish have clean water that is the right temperature, and some plants to hide amongst.

Guinea pigs

Guinea pigs need lots of hay and exercise, as well as a safe, enclosed place with one or more other guinea pigs.

Hamsters

Hamsters are sensitive to high frequency sounds – things such as televisions and vacuum cleaners can disturb them.

Horses and ponies

They need lots of exercise to remain healthy, so access to a big open space or paddock is a must.

Mice

Mice are generally very active at night and like to have lots of places to hide and materials to build nests.

Rabbits

Rabbits will sometimes make a purring noise a bit like a cat if they are happy and content.

Rats

Rats are very sociable and active. To keep them entertained, set up their cage with ropes and other climbing equipment.

Snakes

Snakes shed their skin, so don't be alarmed if you see a long, dry, snake-shaped object in your snake's cage!

Spiders

Most spiders are not sociable animals and should be kept one to a cage, out of direct sunlight.

Stick insects

Stick insects are very delicate and should be handled with great care. They should only live with other stick insects.

Tortoises

Tortoises can live for over 100 years! Make sure they have somewhere to shelter, and plenty of vegetation to eat.